Threads
of
Needlework

Printed by Lulu.com

15384944

and published by Phaselus Publishing

Rhosilli, GU6 8PJ

United Kingdom

phaseluspublishing.wordpress.com

FOREWORD

THREADS of NEEDLEWORK

My family had a long connection with the knit-work and dyeing trades. My paternal grandfather, from Shepshed in Leicestershire, was a hosiery foreman and the last of a long line of frame work knitters; my other grandfather was a dyeing master in Nottingham, succeeded in his post by his son, my uncle. And I have been married for fifty-six years to an enthusiastic and able needlewoman. You may agree that I could hardly ignore the business.

This collection had its origin in a series of essays written twenty or so years ago for the Newsletter of the Kettering Branch of the Embroiderers' Guild. Some years later, two or three were included in the Newsletter of the Guildford Branch.

The original texts have been edited, added to and adapted into this little book in the hope that they will continue to be of interest.

T.M. Cotton
Cranleigh, October 2014

CONTENTS

INTRODUCTION

THERE IS NO REAL distinction underlying the terms 'cloth' and 'fabric', either of which is apt to be called simply 'material' by the user. No matter which term be preferred, there are five well-known methods for making the product: weaving, crochet, lace-making, felting and knitting.

Fabrics are made from threads or yarns from various basic sources, both natural and synthetic, which may be dyed in an infinite variety of colours. This little book briefly describes the production and use of these materials; here, the subject is introduced by reviewing the processes of fabric production, before moving in the following chapters to look at the needle — the basic tool of the trade — and the individual materials concerned.

WEAVING is thought to be an extremely old craft, possibly having been in use for several thousand years. Though it is usually carried out on a loom with movable parts, weaving does not in its basic form require anything more than the simplest of equipment. Described simply, the fabric produced consists of two sets of threads, interlaced at right angles; a loom is a means of holding one set of threads (the *warp*) in place while the second (the *weft*) is passed through them. The principle of a loom is unvarying, whether a basic handicraft tool or a high-speed, mechanised machine.

There are several variations which can be introduced. The use of differently coloured threads to form a regular pattern is an obvious one, while grouping the warp threads, and using combinations of different thread styles in particular ways, can be used to change the fabric's properties from that of plain weaving. Tapestries or carpets use combinations of colour and weaving pattern to produce sometimes spectacular results, and huge areas can be covered.

At the opposite end of the spectrum, woven cloth is used as the substrate for those other kinds of decorative art that are collectively known as needlework. In this respect, a useful characteristic of plain woven material is its resistance to anything more than mild stretching.

In selecting both the fibre from which the fabric is woven and the fineness of the thread itself, the choice of materials is wide. The range of techniques is bewilderingly large: even such a common-place term as embroidery hides a wealth of possibilities — which is to say nothing of patchwork and quilting, where elegant and precise needlework is combined with skilful design and piecing.

CROCHET and LACEMAKING are not often thought of as techniques for making fabric — or at least are regarded as a decorative art that happens to produce something that can, at a pinch, be described as a fabric. Crochet is fairly described as a needlework method, if only because it uses a special, hooked needle; it is usually intended for making a decorative object and is a genuine craft in its own right. Except for enthusiasts, lace-making by hand seems to be a dying art; it was once a significant industry, in Britain mainly centred in Nottingham, but the lace tablecloth is seldom seen nowadays, and the principal modern use of machine-made lace seems to be in trimming ladies' wear.

FELT is a unique kind of fabric, which results from encouraging the natural tendency for fibres and threads to become irretrievably entangled by the application of brute force, lubricated by water. The texture depends greatly on the fineness of the original material; the felt can have anything from a smooth, fine and tough texture, suitable for such as hats and shoes, to something more open, perhaps made by a craft felter for an artistic purpose. Industrially, felt can be produced in flat, wide sheets that can be adapted to various uses; but however it be formed, it is of special interest to the needleworker, who can transform it into useful and decorative objects by skilful cutting, stitching and embroidery.

KNITTED FABRIC is formed by systematically interweaving consecutive rows of a single length of yarn. It is a basic alternative to weaving, one which in its simplest form requires no equipment more complicated than long needles. Knitted fabric is much more elastic than woven cloth, and so is suitable for close-fitting items such as gloves, stockings and T-shirts. While no individual can be identified as the inventor of that other significant means of fabric production, the loom, the inventor of the first knitting machine is known.

Hand-knitting large quantities of garments is laborious: hand-knitting stockings for a population of a few million was never a commercial proposition. This led William Lee, a clergyman of Calverton in Nottinghamshire in the reign of Elizabeth I (and so well before the industrial revolution), to invent the frame work knitting machine — as legend has it, so that his wife (or perhaps his lady-love) might devote more time to him, and less to knitting. The Queen, fearing for the livelihood of the nation's hand-knitters, refused a patent to Lee who, in fine British tradition, went abroad for encouragement, with his brother. The French King Henri IV proved more accommodating.

Lee's machine made flat, plain knitting at eight stitches to the inch and a foot wide. After William died in 1610, his brother returned to London to manufacture silk hose by machine. The process was widely adopted and a Guild was formed. The Civil War caused a migration to the East Midlands, an area already known for hand-knitting. Improvement by Jedediah Strutt in 1758 turned Lee's frame into a complex machine, said to comprise some 3,500 parts.

The Land Enclosures forced many of the agricultural unemployed into frame work knitting, to the extent that by 1800 there were in the East Midlands about 40,000 frames —about 90% of those in the whole country. Interestingly enough, a small pocket of the industry was set up in the Surrey town of Godalming.

The industry's social status did not match its practical success. The machines themselves were extremely expensive and had to be hired from wealthy investors; the frame rents, coupled with derisory piece-rates and liability for repairs, made the name of frame work knitter into a by-word for poverty. Frame work knitting, while continuing as a cottage industry, declined throughout the nineteenth century, slumping, after the fashion changed from knee-breeches to trousers, just about until its end; a few frames were then kept on for sentiment's sake until the 1980s. A heavy blow in 1864 was William Cotton's invention of a so-called straight-bar machine, on which fully-fashioned stockings were made, eliminating all the previous effort and waste of cutting and piecing.

In the nineteenth century this was the last of the fabric production techniques to be fully mechanised. Inevitably, the search for improved efficiency and changes in fashion led to decline. Wool and worsted have virtually disappeared from Leicestershire, silk stockings in Derbyshire and Nottinghamshire have given way to nylon; but it remains a tribute to William Lee that his principle, remarkably enough, is still recognisable in all modern knitwear machinery.

* * *

ALTHOUGH some specialized techniques have been casualties over the years, it is inconceivable that the manufacture of fabrics will ever cease. In one form or another, the use of fabric, and even decorated fabric, has been traced back for thousands of years. The use of fabric is a fundamental part of human history, and we shall go on to look at the sources of our materials, their development into useful products and the improvements in their treatment. But we begin with the needle — their most useful, indeed essential, adjunct.

1. NEEDLES

THERE IS AN OLD STORY that the cities of Birmingham and Sheffield competed in a test of their craftsmen's skills. The tiny life-size, clockwork, articulated spider seemed to have the edge, until Sheffield's needle was unscrewed in the middle, to reveal a second needle inside, which also unscrewed ...

On the basis of craft antiquity, the needle would certainly have carried the day. From sheer necessity, needles must have been first used in stitching clothing. Our ancestors might have spun thread, woven cloth and dressed animal skins: but how would they join pieces together, if not by sewing? The decoration of articles must also date from the very distant past. Although examples of the needle are plentiful, stitched items preserved from antiquity are few. The Romans certainly practised the art of embroidery (in Latin, *acu pingere* — to depict or paint by needle). In Britain, examples exist which pre-date the Conquest and are seen to be very delicately worked, and France has, of course, the largest and most famous European example at Bayeux — a crewel embroidery, worked entirely by needle.

There are (or have been) needles for many purposes: straight, curved, hollow, hooked, sharpened, with or without eyes, of metal, bone, wood or plastic, and round or oval in section. Not all are intended for handicrafts; but they all have one thing in common, that they are smooth, and of precise manufacture. They are nowadays mass-produced, but are still almost works of art in their own right.

The first needles were of bone or ivory, materials not too difficult to work and polish (though extremely good eyesight must have been a prime qualification for the task). Later, craftsmen skilled in metal-working would find fabrication a little easier, being able to form the eye by wrapping a loop at the end of a wire and beating into shape. But hand manufacture would always be slow and laborious, and the product costly and (unless of metal) fragile, with a limited life.

Needles were once manufactured throughout England. A Guild of Needlemakers was eventually incorporated in London in 1656, but during the nineteenth century, while the industrial revolution was everywhere bringing changes to ways of life, the trade mainly settled at Redditch in Worcestershire. There were new sources of power, new machines and manufacturing ideas, and above all there was steel. Commercial knitwear manufacture depended on the intricately shaped 'bearded' needles, which could now be supplied in bulk, and in a durable material. An article once treasured had become an inexpensive trifle. Today, needles are cheap, common-place, and virtually unregarded: it is the use of thread that we admire. Sewing was traditionally a woman's work, and we know (for spinsters are on the distaff side) that women also used to spin the wool or flax: seldom do we think of the implement made by artisans, yet the needle, without which the thread is nothing, is itself a work of extreme craftsmanship.

Think what is required. For hand-knitting or crochet, the material is less important than that for use in a machine, and well-finished wood, bone or plastic is suitable. For everything else, however, the needle must be of hard metal, and sharp, strong, smooth and clean. It must not wear out too quickly. It must not bend under the force of being pushed through the material. And the finer the thread, the more easily is it torn or broken: the value of a needle is nothing if the hole is rough, or has sharp edges. Dickens, in *A Christmas Carol*, speaks of 'the sharpest needle, best Whitechapel, warranted not to cut in the eye'.

A bewildering variety of hand sewing-needles became available: as well as the general purpose 'sharps', the modern tailor or embroiderer can choose needles straight or curved, blunt or sharp, of lengths, thicknesses and hole sizes to suit the particular task. The gleaming, perfectly-formed object that we accept so easily has been drawn into wire from a carefully-chosen grade of steel, straightened, cut, ground, stamped, hardened, tempered, scoured and polished; if it is for a sewing machine, there is the added requirement for a precisely formed shaft.

Next time you pick up a needle, perhaps you will spare a moment to think of its honourable place among mankind's most beneficial inventions, and of the ingenuity that makes a commonplace of such a perfect creation.

2. SPUN THREAD

Allll NEEDLEWORK, like all fabric, depends on spun fibre, whether it be the thread passed through the needle's eye, or knitted into a garment, or woven into cloth which is to be cut, stitched and decorated to make something useful or elegant. In ancient times, when mankind lived much closer to Nature and spinning was a common duty of many women, the Greeks were not alone in regarding this process as symbolic of the life-cycle and, according to one version, believed that there were three *Moirai*, or Fates: Clotho who spun the thread of life, Lachesis who determined its length, and Atropos, who cut it off.

Although modern machinery is complicated and the introduction of synthetic fibre strands — which are uniform, clean and of unrestricted length — has eased the production process, the principles used in forming thread are unchanged from those of antiquity. Thread made from such natural materials as silk, wool, cotton and flax still requires that the material be specially prepared by removing foreign matter and natural contaminants before it can be converted to its final form.

The cleaned fibres had to be teased out in the traditional process — now called 'carding' — of pulling across, for example, dried heads of the plant teasel, to make them lie mainly parallel in a thin sheet; this could then be rolled and pulled into a thick, untwisted and uniform strand, ready for spinning. If the aim was a very fine thread, the shortest fibres were combed out and discarded to leave just the longer ones, which bond more strongly. At this point, the traditional spinster wound the strand round her distaff, from which the thread was drawn out and twisted by the fall of a weighted, whirling spindle.

The spinning wheel, introduced from India and elsewhere to Europe in the Middle Ages, mechanised the process for the first time. The laborious and irregular twirling of the spindle was replaced by the turning wheel, with the new yarn being hand-fed on to the spindle as the wheel turned in the opposite direction. The operation was easier, quicker and tidier, and the quality was more predictable — though it must still have been rather clumsy and laborious.

Modern machinery has been developed since the sixteenth century, when continuous spinning was first made possible by the so-called Saxony wheel, driven by a treadle. Real increases in production speed and scale came with Hargreaves' spinning jenny (1770), followed by Arkwright's enhancements and the vast improvement of Crompton's 'mule' (1779), which allowed a single worker to operate a thousand spindles. Modern machines have devices to draw out the strands to make them longer and thinner, while the spindles deliver the proper amount of twist to suit the material being spun, making for uniformity and adjusting qualities such as strength and elasticity to suit the intended use of the yarn.

Spinning is a technology which has been advanced enormously by the development of treatments for natural materials (for example, 'mercerisation') and the manufacture of such synthetics as nylon and terylene, which can be extruded into strands directly suitable for spinning. It seems unlikely, though, that the natural materials obtained from sustainable resources will ever be completely displaced: there will always be a place, for example, for the element of luxury conferred by silk, or the rugged qualities of wool and linen. Whatever the source, we should, perhaps, occasionally pause to remember with gratitude the inventions that have put the needle-worker's materials within such wide and easy reach.

3. DYES AND DYEING

T HE ADDING OF COLOUR to spun thread or woven cloth is an ancient process. Some dyes from antiquity are well known: yellow saffron and the imperial colour 'Tyrian purple' (derived from a shellfish, and really more red than purple) of the Romans are two such, but each of these is both spectacular and costly in comparison with the more usual colours obtainable from many common plants. We can be pretty sure that the very first dyestuffs, such as woad, were all coloured extracts obtained from plants, either by squeezing out the juice of berries or by macerating and boiling plant fibres with water.

The problem with some crude vegetable dyes was the lack of fastness: they would be removed too easily by washing. Somehow or other, it was discovered that the alkali present in fire-ash, extracted by boiling with water, could sometimes help the process; this may very well have been mankind's first-ever artificial chemical, still sometimes called soda-ash (though it is now produced by other means). Bleachers and dyers had to make do with crude treatments depending on this and other natural products until about 1800, when the chemical industry began as a necessary part of the industrial revolution: indeed, it can be argued that improvement in the bleaching of fabrics was the start, while dyeing was the spur to development of the modern chemical industry.

Chemistry developed only slowly until the mid-nineteenth century, until which time the view had not yet been wholly abandoned that living organisms were the only possible source for carbon-based substances — whose study was, in consequence, known as 'organic chemistry' (as it still is). The first chemical factories were adjuncts to the old-fashioned gasworks for producing gas and coke, which also gave rise to by-products including an ammoniacal liquor and coal tar, each soon discovered to be both complex and valuable. Messy and dirty as it was, coal-tar was the improbable source for the first artificial dye, discovered accidentally in 1858 by a young English chemist, W.H. (later, Sir William) Perkin while investigating a substance, aniline, that he had obtained from it. That dye was *mauve*; a little later came other aniline dyes including *magenta* (named after a battle of 1859, fought during the struggle for the unification of Italy) and *aniline black*. As time went by, study revealed the existence of several, quite different classes of dyestuff which remain useful to this day.

Each different kind of dyestuff and fabric requires its own technique for successful application, though almost every fabric can be dyed at any stage of production, from spinning stock to woven material. Some, not now regarded as true dyes, work by simple staining; they are seldom permanent, tending to be easily removed by washing and to fade in sunlight. Many can be used only in combination with other chemicals. Some do not dissolve in water, but have first to be converted to a different form, which is changed to the desired colour only after it has been applied.

Permanence is, of course, a very desirable feature in a dye; a modern dyeworks has various methods for achieving this. A trick established early on was that of *mordanting*, originally used on natural materials, when a chemical such as alum was first applied to prepare the material so that the dye would 'take' on the treated surface of the fibres. In the nineteen-fifties, so-called reactive dyes were added to the earlier types, being first used on cellulose, where — unlike dyes that require a mordant — they attach themselves directly to the fibres and confer a high degree of colour-fastness.

Various national and international organisations have tried to set standards for colour and fastness, but these can only judge the result of dyeing an actual batch and say nothing about the way that the effect should be achieved. Even with the aid of modern technology, the practice of dyeing retains a degree of craft — most especially where natural fibres are used. The fact that ranges of reliably coloured thread are nowadays at an embroiderer's disposal owes not a little to the benefits of large-scale production, but a great deal also to the skill used by the dyeing master in selecting, preparing and treating the fibre employed.

4. WOOL

IT'S NOT HARD TO SEE why sheepskins should have been prized for the warmth and protection that they gave. More than that, however, the fleece itself is an obvious source of fibre for spinning and weaving, perhaps also for felting. Further, it is unnecessary to kill the animal when just its wool is needed: conveniently enough, it needs only to be sheared regularly for its fleece (usually of eight or nine pounds weight), while the creatures' herd instinct makes for easy control, so that they can be driven to suitable pasture, whether by nomadic herdsmen, or by settled farmers.

The origins of sheep-herding undoubtedly lie in far antiquity so that, for at least seven thousand years, these animals have provided mankind with meat, with leather, and particularly with this wonderful third product, wool. There are many breeds of sheep that may be raised principally for wool in a wide range of climatic conditions: in Britain from the long-haired (Cotswold, Leicester, Romney) and medium-haired (Southdown, Suffolk, Hampshire) English breeds to the fine-wool types that are all descended from the Spanish merino. And when thinking of wool, we should not forget other animals which bear it: the goat, for instance, is the source of cashmere, the finest of all wools that has enjoyed a fashionable vogue as pashmina.

Woollen yarn (so named: the term *thread* is mainly reserved for finer yarns that are used for sewing) is produced in a wide range of thicknesses, according to its source and the intended use, which may range from the hard-wearing, woven worsted and serge to the softest lambswool designed for hand or machine knitting. Embroidery makes its own demands on wool: for example, a very soft embroidery wool, dyed in Germany to very bright colours, enjoyed widespread popularity in the nineteenth century, giving its name to Berlin wool-work.

Woollen yarn is the normal medium for needlepoint, while crewel is a two-ply worsted yarn, constantly in fashion for the last four hundred years for working on a ground of linen, cotton or twill (and, of course, every embroiderer worthy of the name knows that the Bayeux Tapestry is really a crewel-work in wool, not woven but stitched by needle).

The prosperity of England in medieval times arose in large part from its wool and woollen products. So profitable was the business that in East Anglia, the major producing region, it was not unknown for the population to be driven out to make way for grazing — a harshly cruel measure that was later to find an echo in the Highland clearances. Any guilt that may have been felt by the wool magnates seems to have been expiated in church-building: many a village of Norfolk and Suffolk can boast a splendid edifice, built on the profits from the trade: we may, indeed, reflect on the fact that, even today, many are the kneelers, worked in woollen cross-stitch, that are found in such places.

The trade in the middle ages was actually run at local production centres by the merchant guilds, which controlled the buying and selling of raw wool as well as finished products; it was supplied through the physical work of carding, weaving and so on that was undertaken by the craft guilds. The main period of prosperity lasted from the late thirteenth century until the eighteenth; this period of successful wool business not only gave spectacular profits to its entrepreneurs, but was one of the most important sources of revenue for the Crown — so much so that the revenues raised were marked by the Woolsack on which the Lord Chancellor traditionally sat in the House of Lords.

5. LINEN

M UCH OF ENGLAND has become accustomed, through recent decades, to fields disfigured by the unsightly, strident yellow of oil-seed rape. Just occasionally, however, is seen a gentler, visually more attractive crop — the blue flower of flax, commoner in the cooler, more moist conditions found in the north of Ireland than on the British mainland, and a plant unusual in being grown (according to variety) for either of two important products. From its botanical name *linum* are derived the names of linseed, from which the oil is extracted, and linen, for which yarn and fabric are made from the stem fibres. The oil has special drying qualities which make it a suitable medium for paint; the fibre is the basis of one of the oldest of textile products.

There is some evidence that linen was used in extreme antiquity, but the surviving early examples of actual, fine linen cloth are later, coming from ancient Egyptian tombs of perhaps 5,000 years ago. It is believed that Phœnician traders carried the material around the Mediterranean, and the Romans later promoted its manufacture throughout their Empire. Since those distant times, the importance of linen may have diminished, but it has never ceased.

The plant is generally suitable for the cooler, northerly climates, so that it has often been a major crop from the Netherlands and Germany across to Russia, and in Japan. Flax grown for fibre is densely planted to encourage tall, straight growth to a height of three or four feet. When the fruit has set, but before the seeds are mature, the slender stems are harvested to be converted into fibre.

The processing is fairly brutal, involving soaking, drying, crushing and beating, but so tough is the fibre that strands of between twelve and thirty inches are obtained, easily spun into a hard, durable thread of the familiar 'unbleached linen' colour.

Although linen is valued for its smoothness, strength and durability, and may be bleached to a pure white, it does not easily take dyes; and it compares poorly with other natural fibres in everyday use such as wool and cotton in being not very elastic, and creasing readily. As a result, it is valued more as yarn or canvas. The greater proportion of modern 'bed-linen' owes nothing more to the material than its name: and, although linen fabric is still employed to some extent in tailoring, it has been displaced in this and similar uses by materials which can be more readily dyed. Lace of very high quality can be made from linen yarn, and the toughness of the linen thread used for twine, in fishnetting and in industrial sewing is legendary, but its interest in needlework is virtually limited to using the cloth as a ground material.

The strength and stretching resistance of linen material makes it an excellent, practical ground for such as altar frontals, but it is now seldom, in fact, much embroidered for anything but formal articles. This was not always so: fifty years ago it was still a regular basis for hand-worked table-cloths, tray-cloths, antimacassars and similar household articles, where patterns and pictures would be worked in silks, often to an ironed-on commercial pattern. Black-work, white-work and cut-work are all still practised on a linen base, though they are in truth minority interests, even if the results are often very attractive. Even linen canvas is being partly supplanted by an alternative of plastic mesh.

Will linen ever regain more than its present 'interesting, but only occasionally useful' status among embroiderers? With the easy availability of so many modern alternatives, this may be doubted. Nevertheless, it is pleasing to find that the malodorous yellow fields of the contemporary countryside can still be relieved by the occasional sea of blue flax-blossom.

6. SILK

ILK, SO MUCH PRIZED for its proverbial smoothness, obtainable in a variety of forms and still often favoured by embroiderers, is a remarkable material from an unlikely source. It is produced by an industry that has often been secretive, occasionally at hazard through natural causes, and so furnishing interesting parallels to rubber and wine, two other staples of modern times.

It's easy enough to imagine that wool might be clipped from sheep and turned into thread: after all, it somehow looks the part. Nor is it too difficult to discover that the stems of plants contain long, tough fibres. Plants and sheep abound, and quantity is hardly a problem. But how did the fine, fragile thread, spun into a cocoon by the larva of a moth that seems to live only on mulberry leaves, ever come to be the basis of such a great and valuable industry, with an annual output once measured in hundreds of tons?

No one disputes that the discovery happened in China, where records suggest that silk was being produced as long ago as five thousand years, but do not identify the genius who discovered how to unwind half a mile of fragile filament and turn it into useful thread (and so provided an early and compelling illustration of Edison's dictum that 'genius is one percent inspiration, ninety-nine percent perspiration').

Nevertheless, the discovery was made, the thread was spun and woven, and silk cloth was exported as far as India and Persia during the first millennium BC. Despite the secrecy practised by the Chinese, the techniques of rearing the silkworm and spinning from its larva spread to India, from where exports began in the second century BC. For the five hundred years up to AD250, Persia was the major trading centre for silk.

Silk dyeing and weaving were both developed throughout the lands surrounding the eastern Mediterranean; and, though it seems that they often had to get their yarn for sewing by laboriously unravelling the imported cloth, they must eventually have gained access to some sources of spun thread for weaving, if not for the actual spinning.

Of course, the culture did not remain secret for ever and, just as the seeds of the rubber tree were later smuggled out of Brazil to start a worldwide industry, so the origin of sericulture in Europe was said to have been silkworms illicitly imported to Constantinople in about AD550 by two Persian monks. The industry settled mainly in France and Italy, where it flourished until the great silkworm plague of 1854, during the period in which phylloxera was devastating the wine industry. The cause of the silkworm plague was found in 1865 by Louis Pasteur, who was able to propose a means of control; sadly, it was too late to save silk production in his own country, although there was a satisfactory recovery in Italy.

Silk and silk products also formed an industry at scattered English locations, dating back to the earlier eighteenth century, which survives in a few places even in the current decade; it is commemorated in several museums, but actual silk weaving is now almost entirely confined to the area around Sudbury in Suffolk.

Such are the qualities of silk that the industry has survived the introduction of cheaper modern substitutes such as rayon and nylon; but inevitably, though it is still important in the Far East, production in the United Kingdom is much reduced. Silk is, of course, a delicate material that eventually wears and decays more rapidly than less exotic alternatives. It is still valued for its intrinsic qualities and is not, in fact, so expensive as to be reserved only to use in so-called luxury goods; and, fortunately, it appears likely to remain available as one of the embroiderer's options.

7. COTTON

I T'S NO SURPRISE to learn that most agriculture is devoted to growing foodstuffs: but the most important crop that is not grown for food is neither timber nor tobacco, as might be expected, but cotton. The cultivation of cotton is of great antiquity, and has spread right around the world: given suitable soil and adequate water, it can be grown anywhere within about 2,000 miles of the equator (which is 3,670 miles south of London — so unless global warming gets a move on, it's not likely to become a British product to rival wool or flax).

The cotton plant grows to between four and six feet to produce triangular seed-pods. The pod, or boll, bursts open to reveal a white, fluffy mass. This contains the seeds, which have attached hairs that may be almost three inches long, known as lint, and are accompanied by a second, shorter growth called linters. No natural source of fibre is without its problems, and cotton is subject to a good many insect pests as well as vagaries of the weather. As a source of fibre, it is nearly on a par with wool in being more immediately spinnable than flax and silk; while, in contrast with wool, it does not depend on the raising of animals, with the attendant difficulties of finding pasture, over-wintering and so on.

Unless caused by deliberate action for commercial advantage, world shortages in the cotton trade are rare, if only because there are almost always significant production areas where cotton can be found growing free of difficulties. Before the spinning, the process of turning the fibres into yarn is largely a matter of removing the seeds (as much as two-thirds of the initial crop weight) and cleaning the fibrous residue (although mechanised suction-picking is faster, it picks up dust and debris, while hand-picking gives a cleaner crop, in which selection according to ripeness ensures a higher yield).

The greatest invention in processing was Whitney's cotton gin, introduced in the USA in 1793 and a significant contribution to the Industrial Revolution. This ingenious machine made possible the efficient separation of the fibres from the seeds, enormously increasing productivity and ensuring that cotton in the American South thereafter predominated over tobacco as a cash crop. Its political effect was disastrous for the South in the lead-up to the American Civil War, for the southern states wrongly believed that no opponent would dare wage war and so put 'King Cotton' at risk.

Cotton goods were a significant product in Britain too, where the trade settled west of the Pennines in the hinterland of the developing port of Liverpool, and of Manchester at the end of its ship canal. The local climate was ideal, importing and transport had few problems, and the great Lancashire cotton textile industry readily came into being.

It is arguable that cotton is one of mankind's greater natural benefits. It is an eminently renewable resource, available from a broad enough swathe of the Earth's populated regions to insulate it in general from politics and all but a world-wide natural disaster. At maybe a hundred million tons per year, it hardly seems likely that oil-based polymers will ever supplant more than a fraction of production. And we can be sure that, whether as stranded thread or as a cloth base, no embroiderer will ever find supplies of cotton running out.

8. CANVAS

THAT WELL-KNOWN — and widely popular — kind of embroidery called 'canvas work' has an innocent enough name. Or has it? For your dictionary may tell you that *canvas* is a corruption of the Latin word for hemp — which is *cannabis*. Might we be heading for murky waters if we pursue the subject too vigorously?

Well, not really. The hemps are mostly plants which, along with the hops used in brewing, belong either to the nettle family or the mulberries, according to choice, and it is true enough that they include the plants that yield marijuana. However, the overwhelming bulk of the crop is grown for neither oilseed nor drugs, but for fibre, and we can be pretty sure that the canvas used for, say, a kneeler in our local church is innocent of all connection with the less reputable side of the industry. In fact, the name hemp is given to several quite unrelated plants, of which only one is an effective source for the narcotic; for instance, the so-called Indian hemp of North America was certainly used by the native Americans as a source of fibre and is still widely cultivated, but it is not of the real hemp family.

The authentic hemp plant had its origins in central Asia. Like so much else, the cultivation of hemp for its fibre began in China — probably around 2,800 BC. The plants reach heights up to nine feet, with straight stems; after cropping they are soaked, dried, crushed and shaken free of the woody part. The result is fibres of up to six feet in length. The product, as might be expected, somewhat resembles flax, but it is harder, coarser and difficult to bleach and so is usually destined for coarser materials than linen, such as burlap, canvas, rope and string. An exception to the general run of treatment is found in Italy, where special processing gives fibre of an attractive, off-white colour that can be used to simulate linen — although, with flax so readily available, one may wonder at anyone taking the trouble.

But looking further into the matter, we find that hemp is just one of several fibres that may be used in the manufacture of canvas and, in fact, 'canvas' has become merely the generic name for fairly coarse, often thick but always tough cloth, which may contain flax, cotton, jute, or mixtures of these with each other, or with the (cannabis) hemp that gave the product its name. The yarns used in making canvas are always of at least two-ply, which ensures that irregularities tend to even themselves out, and so to give a uniform thickness. For the 'open' canvas familiar to embroiderers, a special weaving pattern is necessary, differentiating this use from almost all others, such as sailcloth, tarpaulin and artists' canvas. Least of all is the embroiderer likely to thread a needle with a yarn having any content of hemp: plainly, with this particular fibre, we are at the very edge of our interest (unless, perhaps, we are unfortunate enough to be sewing mailbags as a guest of Her Majesty) as far as actual needlework is concerned.

9. SYNTHETIC FIBRES

THE EIGHTEEN-FIFTIES, marked by the birth of the synthetic dye, were a crucial period in the development of chemistry, which had really begun to appear in its modern form at the time of the French Revolution and now gained the attention of some of the great names in its history. Chemistry is traditionally divided into three main branches, one being called 'organic chemistry,' the source of all the modern discoveries in synthetic materials including pharmaceuticals, dyes and plastics, and thus the provider of, *inter alia*, the vast modern range of coloured threads, yarns and fabrics.

Modern dyestuffs were intended in the first instance only for application to natural fibres — wool, silk, flax etc. — which were at the time still the only source of yarns and fabrics. The earliest attempts to improve quality in the thread itself led to the process of *mercerisation*, invented by an English calico printer, John Mercer, in 1844 and patented in 1850. It is a simple chemical process, mainly used on high-quality cotton goods, that improves not only the fibre strength (and thus the resistance to wear), but also the brightness and colour-fastness of the dyes that are then applied.

Rather more ambitious than mercerisation was the attempt to produce an artificial silk ('wood-silk') from the cellulose of which all plant fibres consist. The first successful technique dates from 1890, and was an authentic chemical process, developed in Germany, that transformed the original material into continuously spun fibre, known as 'Bemberg'. This was rapidly followed in 1892 by viscose yarn, so called because the original fibre was converted to a treacly solution that could be spun, rather as a spider spins its web. In 1924, these cellulose-based yarns became collectively known as *rayon*, by which time the treatment and production possibilities were becoming more and more extensive.

One advantage of rayon products lies in the efficient conversion of the natural material, without having to reject a large proportion of short fibre. However, it still relies on the cropping of trees and plants, with the attendant difficulties of bulk transportation, sorting and cleaning before proper processing can begin. The situation changed radically with the arrival of completely synthetic materials, loosely known as plastics, that were derived from petroleum-based chemicals. Petroleum is itself a complex natural product, entirely a mixture of 'organic' hydrocarbon compounds; it is now the basis for the familiar products of the polymer industry such as nylon, terylene and polythene, many of which can be spun into filaments that are suitable for the manufacture of yarns and fabrics.

Nylon, itself invented in 1924, is of a type ('polyamide') differing from the polyesters (such as terylene): but all modern synthetic fibres can be formed into regular strands of precise thickness and extreme length, from which yarn can be formed without the kind of spinning that is necessitated by the staple lengths of most natural fibres. Terylene was discovered in England during the nineteen-forties at the Calico Printers' Association, but wartime secrecy delayed production by ICI until 1954. The similar Dacron was produced a year earlier than that in the USA.

The yarns and textiles of today seem almost limitless in their variety of colour, light-fastness and strength, gained by using combinations of synthetic with natural fibres which can add a welcome degree of wear-resistance, strength and elasticity. Even so, while modern materials are welcomed for the advantages they bring, traditionalists may be happy to recognise that the use of natural fibres continues, and embroiderers may smile at the thought that interest in their craft materials was a catalyst at the birth of a great industry.